ZiGGYS
OF THE WORLD
UNiTE!

More Humor from SIGNET

ZiGGYS OF THE WORLD UNiTE!

BY Tom Wilson

A SIGNET BOOK

NEW AMERICAN LIBRARY

TIMES MIRROR

for YOU
my ZIGGY FRIEND!

ZiGGYS
OF THE WORLD
UNiTE!

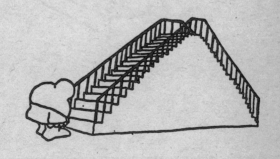

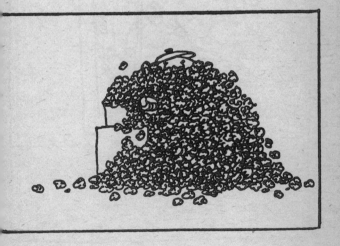

ACCORDING TO
MEDICAL SCIENCE
i REACHED MY
ENERGY PEAK
3 YEARS AGO...

...i MUSTA
SLEPT THROUGH IT.

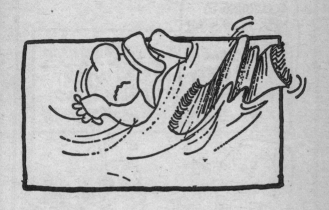

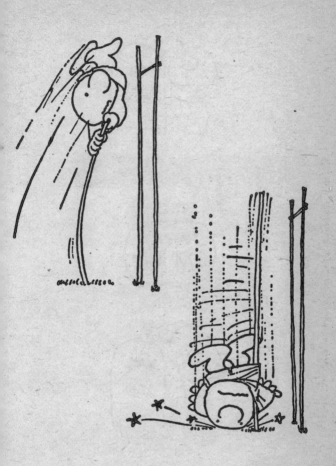

SOMEONE TOLD
ME THAT IF i PUT
A PENNY IN MY
SHOE IT WOULD
BRING ME GOOD
LUCK ...
SO i TRIED IT..

...GOT THE BIGGEST
BLISTER YOU EVER
SAW !!

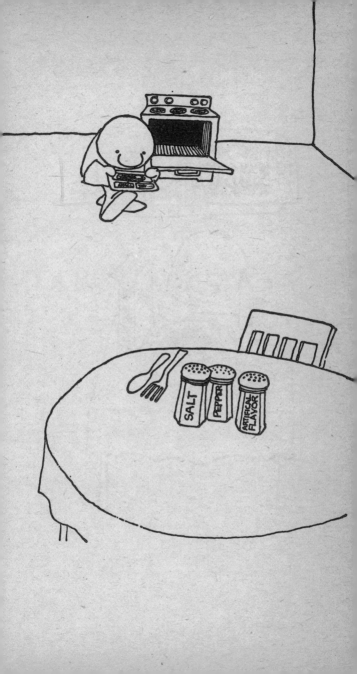

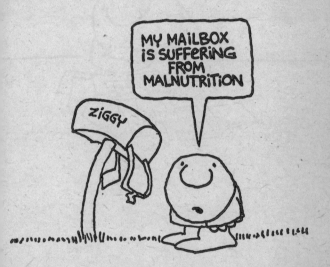

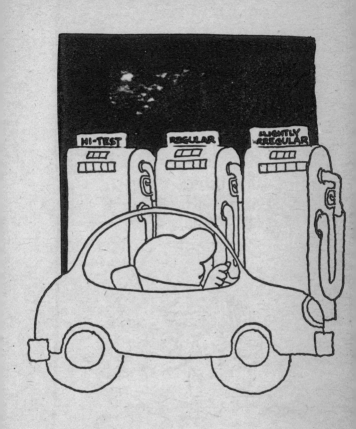

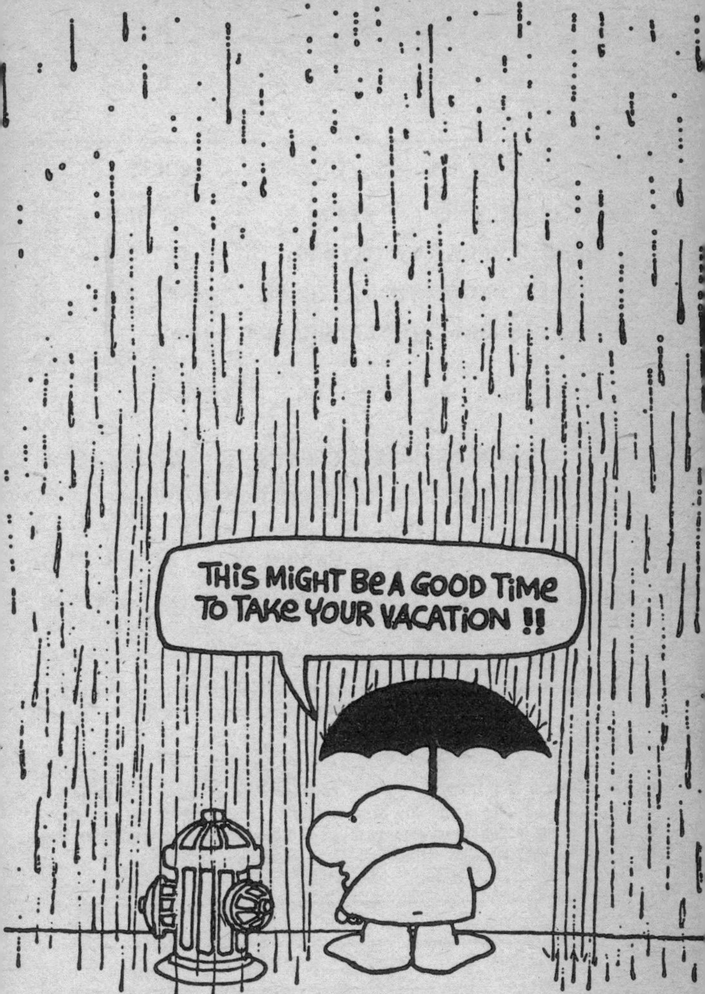
THIS MIGHT BE A GOOD TIME TO TAKE YOUR VACATION !!

SIGNET Peanuts Books by Charles M. Schulz

MAD Humor from SIGNET

by Don Martin

☐ **MAD'S DON MARTIN COOKS UP MORE TALES**
(#Q6295—95¢)
☐ **MAD'S DON MARTIN COMES ON STRONG** (#Y6854—$1.25)
☐ **MAD'S DON MARTIN BOUNCES BACK** (#Q6294—95¢)

by David Berg

☐ **MAD'S DAVE BERG LOOKS AT OUR SICK WORLD**
(#Y7014—$1.25)
☐ **MAD'S DAVE BERG LOOKS AT THE U.S.A.** (#Y6978—$1.25)
☐ **MAD'S DAVE BERG LOOKS AT MODERN THINKING**
(#Q6630—95¢)
☐ **MAD'S DAVE BERG LOOKS AT THINGS** (#T5070—75¢)
☐ **ROGER KAPUTNIK AND GOD** (#Y8153—$1.25)

by William Gaines

☐ **GOOD 'N' MAD** (#Q6342—95¢)
☐ **GREASY MAD STUFF** (#Q6499—95¢)
☐ **HOPPING MAD** (#Q6291—95¢)
☐ **MAD POWER** (#Y6741—$1.25)
☐ **THE PORTABLE MAD** (#Y6742—$1.25)
☐ **SELF-MADE MAD** (#Y6981—$1.25)
☐ **THE THREE RING MAD** (#Y6917—$1.25)
☐ **THE VOODOO MAD** (#Q6245—95¢)

Buy them at your local
bookstore or use coupon
on next page for ordering.